America's Star-Spangled Story

JANE HAMPTON COOK

To Bunny —
God Bless America!
Jane Hampton Cook

Lighthouse Publishing
of the Carolinas

PRAISE FOR *AMERICA'S STAR-SPANGLED STORY*

Inspiring and important. History every American should know told in a way everyone will enjoy. Delightful and fascinating. A joy to read.

~ Jocelyn Green
Award-winning author of *Stories of Faith and Courage from the Home Front* and *Heroines Behind the Lines* Civil War series

AMERICA'S STAR-SPANGLED STORY BY JANE HAMPTON COOK
Published by Lighthouse Publishing of the Carolinas
2333 Barton Oaks Dr., Raleigh, NC, 27614

ISBN: 1941103391
ISBN-13: 978-1941103395
Copyright © 2014 by Jane Hampton Cook
Cover design by Jane Hampton Cook.
Cover photo credits: Fireworks at Fort McHenry, US Navy, and the Star-Spangled Banner Flag, Smithsonian Institution Archives, Wikimedia Commons Public Domain.
Photos are public domain except for those taken by Jane Hampton Cook, Jennifer Davis Heffner, and Paul Ernest.

Available in print from your local bookstore, online, or from the publisher at: www.lighthousepublishingofthecarolinas.com

For more information on this book and the author visit: www.janecook.com

Scripture comes from the New International Version (NIV®), by The Zondervan Corporation, L.L.C., except for Matthew 5:14, which is the King James Version and in the public domain.

Library of Congress Cataloging-in-Publication Data
Cook, Jane Hampton
America's Star-Spangled Story / Jane Hampton Cook 1st ed.

Printed in the United States of America

Dedicated in memory of my mother,
Judith Travis Hampton, whose love of
the flag led her to sew numerous quilts
featuring the stars and stripes.

Acknowledgments

First, many thanks belongs to Eddie Jones, Michele Creech, and the team at Lighthouse Publishing of the Carolinas for your cutting edge, practical approach to modern-day publishing. Thanks as well to my terrific, top notch agent, Jonathan Clements, for keeping an eagle eye out for me.

I also want to recognize and thank my "Star-Spangled Story" editorial team: John Kim Cook, Lorraine Kuchmy, K'Lynn Edwards, Wendy Fotopoulos, Greg Davidson, Lois Ferguson, John Choins, Scarlett Royce, Chrissy Frank, Skyla Frank, Natalie Scholl, Karen Weik, Heather Enright, Grace Coopman, Savonne Caughey, Jocelyn Green, Denny Hartford, Clayton Olson, Jayne Young, Contessa Desser, Randy Huntley, Mary Martin, Tom Parsons, Brigid Hasson, Sarah Blanchard, and Connie Marshner,

I so appreciate my dear mother, Judy Travis Hampton, who passed away in May 2014 while this book was in development. She always supported my talents, and I now especially treasure her talent and the many patriotic flag quilts that she made over the years. Ever grateful for the support and love of my husband, John Kim Cook, I appreciate our family trips to Baltimore, where our sons have heard the story about the anthem of the ages.

Contents

Sailing ships kick off the Star-Spangled Sailabration, Baltimore, June 2012 © Jane Hampton Cook, www.janecook.com.

There is a secret in life .... we all have a
great hand in the forming of our own destiny.
~Dolley Madison

— 1 —

O Say Can You See

What comes to mind when you think of our national anthem, *The Star-Spangled Banner*, and the United States of America? Can you see what the song's lyricist, Francis Scott Key, saw? Or do you picture something else on the mural of your patriotic mind? What battlefields from US history tug at your heart? Which blessings shine brightly from freedom's timeline?

What did the Pilgrims see when their buckled boots clicked and clacked onto Plymouth's rocky shores in 1620? Using a spyglass of hope, they saw a land of fertile seed and a place to worship as they pleased. Borrowing from the language of a native tribe, the great hills—*Massawachusett*—became a colony, chartered for the English crown.

Others who settled farther south also saw future cities on hills. They named sapphire rivers and emerald forests for kings and queens of yore, such as Maryland, Georg-ia, and Virgin-ia, after the virgin Queen Elizabeth. Ultimately these settlers gave birth to thirteen new, distinct places.

A century and a half later in 1776, their descendents saw something different in their overseas monarchs. They saw royalty without representa-

tion. Dependence, not independence. Acts of tyranny enough to fill a declaration. They believed that humanity's rights were natural. Intrinsic. Gifts of God and not of man. And so they took to the battlefield to grasp the blessing of liberty. Independence and self-government were their reward.

But in less than forty years, by 1812, freedom was on the line again. Independence was in name only. America was a power, but hardly a super one. US citizens who sailed the open seas were vulnerable to kidnapping. Worse, British captains forced many of them to serve the English prince again in his Royal Navy and Army. Between five and nine thousand men were suppressed through this unjust practice called impressment.

That's what Francis Scott Key saw two hundred years ago. On August 24, 1814, this Washington-area attorney awakened to the news that the red-coated enemy had come again to his country's shores. After winning a nearby battle, British

An engraving depicts Dolley Madison, Library of Congress.

As Dolley Madison evacuated the White House just a few hours before the British burned it on August 24, 1814, she made sure that Gilbert Stuart's painting of George Washington—one of America's rare national treasures—was safely removed and relocated.

soldiers and sailors then torched our nation's capital city on a hill. Blackened debris replaced the grand White House. Burned walls. Charred remains. Stains of soot. The once pillared US Capitol was also a shell of nothingness. Mr. Key feared that his country was almost lost. Yet, he soon had a front row seat as a witness to the battle that would change everything and give our nation its official song.

When sight becomes a gift of beauty and hope, it is called insight. That's what Key would come to see.

The smoldering fires of the Capitol were spices of the phoenix bed, from which arose offspring more vigorous, beautiful, and long lived.   ~Congressman Charles J. Ingersoll

— 2 —

By the Dawn's Early Light

*W*hat do you do at dawn? Shower? Shave? Snooze? Maybe a better question is this: Where does your dawn begin each day? At early light? After sunrise? With the help of an alarm clock? Makeup mirror? Coffee pot? Car?

We each have one, a daily awakening. Sometimes a seemingly ordinary day, however, becomes an awakening to life. Many big events in US history started this way.

One April night in 1775, more than seventy men grabbed their muskets and, within minutes, gathered in Lexington, Massachusetts. The first shot of the American Revolution was fired there around sunrise, when uniformed British soldiers arrived.

Whether Francis Scott Key's awakening came at dawn or later in the day is lost to history. But come it did on September 1, 1814. Maybe it started by reading his hometown newspaper at his house in Georgetown, located just outside of Washington, DC.

Because local residents feared that British forces would return to Washington and also try to conquer other cities, the editors of *The Federal Republican-Georgetown* newspaper issued a call to action on September 1: "Unless the country is to be abandoned by the people ... every man should awake, arouse, and prepare for action." It was time to push the people's panic into productivity.

Or maybe it was a knocking on Key's door that first awakened him. Standing there was a familiar face with an unfamiliar story. One of his brothers-in-law, Richard West, had rushed from Marlboro, Maryland, where the British had camped recently. He explained that their friend, a physician named Dr. William Beanes, had been taken prisoner by Robert Ross, the British general who had burned Washington, DC just a few days earlier.

Unjust it was. As a physician devoted to help those in need, Beanes had opened his home to the British, treated their wounded, and tended their sick. After the troops evacuated Marlboro, one of the British soldiers had stayed behind and threatened local residents. Beanes had merely made a citizen's arrest of someone who was endangering the lives of others. When General Ross heard what happened, he ordered British soldiers to return and seize Dr. Beanes, the Good Samaritan, and imprison him on a British ship.

After telling him the story of Dr. Beanes, Key's brother-in-law asked him a question. Would he intervene for Beanes?

Advocating was what this attorney did best. Over the years Key had helped his clients sell their estates by advertising them, holding public auctions, and certifying the sales. Business had been slow of late. War will do that. So stale had work become that he'd recently written his mother of possibly changing professions.

"I really think I shall try to purchase a small flock of sheep in the spring, and if the war lasts on, I shall be obliged to leave this [Georgetown]... and turn shepherd," he explained.

Yet, at dawn each day this father of eleven children preferred to don the hat of a lawyer, not hold the staff of a herder. "I have not determined upon anything but to stay here and mind my business as long as I can."

☆☆☆☆☆☆☆☆☆☆☆☆☆☆☆☆☆☆☆☆☆☆

When the dawn comes forth I wonder
Will our sad, sad hearts awaken,
And the grief we labored under
From the new-in-joy be shaken?
"Waiting," George William "A. E." Russell
(1867–1935)

☆☆☆☆☆☆☆☆☆☆☆☆☆☆☆☆☆☆☆☆☆☆

Now he could no longer mind his own business. He must advocate for the physician. He would have to leave the comfort and responsibilities of home to do it. He had been awakened to a new dawn's early light.

— 3 —

What So Proudly We Hailed

*P*eople take pride in many things. Houses. Hometowns. Home states. Sometimes pride unites. Together mothers and fathers beam with pride over their children's accomplishments. Colleagues cheer each other and celebrate when their business succeeds.

Sometimes pride divides. High school friends choose different colleges and root against each other for rival teams. Residents of different states boast of better food, scenery, and sports.

American pride can take on many forms and faces: parades, fireworks, Olympic athletes, and military members. When a country goes to war, however, a nation needs unification. But disagreement over a war's necessity can mark the clearest of dividing lines.

As president of the United States, James Madison experienced this problem. When Congress declared war against England in 1812, he told the American people that multiple diplomatic discussions over the issues of impressment and fair trade had failed. In order to survive as a country, America needed to thrive economically. Britain still refused to "yield to the claims of justice or renounce the errors of a false pride." War was the result. The president soon saw that politics divided Americans into supporters and opponents of the first war since the Revolution.

At age sixty-three, Madison had come to power because he had played an important role in forging the US Constitution, a major source of American pride. Hailing from a prominent Virginia farming family, he'd studied law at the college in Princeton, New Jersey, where his mentor was a minister and the college's president.

Though he also came from a farming family, at age thirty-five Francis Scott Key was much younger than the president and took pride in his home state of Maryland. Attending St. John's College in Annapolis, he'd considered becoming a preacher before also finding his calling in the law.

Key had not been a supporter of Mr. Madison's war, however. To one of the president's most vocal opponents, he later complained about the "abominable war." He also abhorred the fact that the start of the war "was received with public rejoicings" in Baltimore, Maryland's largest city.

Within hours of hearing about the arrest of Dr. Beanes on September 1, 1814, Key put aside his political differences and called upon President Madison. Because the White House had been burned, the president and his wife, Dolley, were staying at her sister's Washington, DC townhome.

Key's meeting with the president was productive. Agreeing that Beanes should be released, Madison authorized Key to go to Baltimore to find John Skinner, the military's prisoner of war negotiator. Together they were to embark on a special mission to negotiate a deal for Dr. Beanes with British officers.

Though holding different views on the war, pride in their country united Key and Madison that day. Soon Key would head to Baltimore, along with thousands of others hailing from different towns but proudly united in defeating the British and saving independence in their wake.

What makes you proud of your country, state, or hometown today?

☆☆☆☆☆☆☆☆☆☆☆☆☆☆☆☆☆☆☆☆☆☆

Children's children are a crown to the aged,
and parents are the pride of their children.
Proverbs 17:6 (NIV)

☆☆☆☆☆☆☆☆☆☆☆☆☆☆☆☆☆☆☆☆☆☆

— 4 —

At the Twilight's Last Gleaming

Sometimes woven into the tapestry of life are threads of ambiguity. They are the "maybe yes, maybe no" moments. Announcements of job layoffs. Rounds of chemotherapy. Competing bids. They are the sweet and sour moments, hinting at both hopeful and fearful outcomes. These can seem like metallic fibers, ones that glimmer in fading light but grow dark with all the others when light is completely absent.

In nature, twilight is the period of time when the sun is below the horizon and the earth's atmosphere refracts its light. This is a soft glowing or half light. Such haziness creates a vague or obscure environment. So it is sometimes in life.

Francis Scott Key spent the next several days living in a twilight of sorts. He had found John Skinner in Baltimore. Together they'd boarded a small boat armed with a flag of truce. Then they navigated the Patapsco, the river leading away from Baltimore, on a mission to find the British fleet. Theirs was an ambiguous journey. Would they be seen as a warship by the enemy? Or would their flag of truce be respected? Would their mission have the desired outcome, releasing Dr. Beanes and returning safely home? Or would they fail and also be captured?

Key and Skinner were aware of the newspapers, which had reported that the commanding British admiral's orders included "destroying and laying waste such towns and districts upon the US coast as may be found assailable." After wandering about in their boat, they encountered a small British vessel called the *Royal Oak*. They hailed it. A discussion ensued.

The *Royal Oak's* captain offered to take them to his leader, Admiral Alexander Cochrane, the commanding admiral who oversaw the entire British fleet. Key and Skinner followed the *Royal Oak*. Finally, right before dinner on September 7, they found it, the admiral's flagship.

What would they discover at the heart of the enemy's fleet? Hostility? Brutality? Contempt? Would their journey send

☆☆☆☆☆☆☆☆☆☆☆☆☆☆☆☆☆☆☆☆☆☆☆☆☆

The day was lingering in the pale northwest,
And light was hanging o'er my head,
Night where a myriad stars were spread;
While down in the east, where the light was
least, Seemed the home of the quiet dead.
"Twilight," Charles Heavysege (1833–1908)

☆☆☆☆☆☆☆☆☆☆☆☆☆☆☆☆☆☆☆☆☆☆☆☆☆

them into further darkness? Would they ever see the dawn?

What do you do when life sends you threads of twilight? Do you hope for the dawn or worry about the darkness ahead? Sometimes days and days must go by before the reality is clear.

TWILIGHT HOVERS OVER WATER. US NATIONAL OCEANIC AND ATMOSPHERIC ADMINISTRATION, WIKIMEDIA COMMONS PUBLIC DOMAIN.

FIFTEEN STARS DOTTED 1812-ERA FLAGS AT THE STAR-SPANGLED SAILABRATION, BALTIMORE, JUNE 2012 © JANE HAMPTON COOK.

However, under a full persuasion of the justice of our cause, I cannot entertain an idea that it [victory] will finally sink, tho' it may remain for some time under a cloud. ~George Washington

— 5 —

Whose Broad Stripes

*W*hat would life be like without symbols? We frequently use simple pictures to show complex ideas. A wedding ring means marriage. Companies use brands to sell their products. Graphic icons hint at something intriguing. A picture on a mobile phone leads to action. Often something small represents something big. A flag represents a nation.

The broad stripes that first greeted Francis Scott Key and John Skinner on September 7, 1814, were hardly glorious. They had reached the *Tonnant*, the British admiral's flagship. Flapping in the breeze were Royal Navy flags. Likely among them was a Union Jack, the United Kingdom's national flag.

By combining the crosses of England and Wales, Scotland, and Ireland, this banner shows centralized royal power. Running across the flag's center is a broad red stripe on a white background, representing the single sovereign who reigns over all of them. Another bold red stripe runs vertically, in the center, to form a cross, suggesting Christianity as the author of the king's or queen's power. Remaining red and white bands diagonally slice blue corners.

Key, of course, embraced different broad stripes. He also knew the power of symbolism. The US flag was a microcosm, a picture, of his beloved native country.

Years earlier, the Continental Congress established America's first symbol of the thirteen colonies turned into states. "That the flag of the thirteen United States be thirteen stripes, alternate red and white," they proclaimed on June 14, 1777.

By Key's day in 1814, the flag featured more red and white stripes than any previous flag—fifteen to represent each state, including the two newest, Vermont and Kentucky.

☆☆☆☆☆☆☆☆☆☆☆☆☆☆☆☆☆☆☆☆☆☆☆☆

Say to them, 'This is what the Sovereign Lord says: A great eagle with powerful wings, long feathers and full plumage of varied colors came to Lebanon ... "
Ezekiel 17:3a (NIV)

☆☆☆☆☆☆☆☆☆☆☆☆☆☆☆☆☆☆☆☆☆☆☆☆

The colors had meaning, too. A few years after issuing the flag, the Continental Congress defined red, white, and blue when it created the official US seal, which features an eagle in the center. Red means hardiness and valor. White means innocence and purity, while blue means vigilance, perseverance, and justice.

The best of banners don't merely represent geography. They depict the source of their power and reveal the type of government they herald. Life would be less meaningful without symbols to inspire us.

A POSTER CELEBRATES FLAG DAY IN 1917, LIBRARY OF CONGRESS.

— 6 —

And Bright Stars

What do you think of when you look at the stars in the sky? To some, stars are God's map, his original GPS or global positioning system for humanity. The wise men followed stars to find the Messiah child. Explorers followed stars to navigate oceans. In the modern day, as in the ancient, the sight of shining stars indicates a cloudless night.

When the Continental Congress created the US flag on June 14, 1777, they used the star to symbolize each of the thirteen states, declaring, "that the union be thirteen stars, white in a blue field, representing a new constellation." Stars also show that the US government derives its power from people—from representation, not royalty.

Tapping symbolism and fearing a British attack in 1776, the residents of Baltimore erected a rustic fort in the shape of a star during the American Revolution. Years later in 1798, authorized by the US Congress, the city hired experienced French engineers to reconstruct Fort McHenry as a formidable protection for Baltimore's harbor. Its location was ideal because it overlooks the Patapsco River, where it divides into two forks, with one leading to the city's commercial harbor.

Just as Key and Skinner boarded the *Tonnant* several miles away on September 7, 1814, Americans back in Baltimore were preparing for action. General Samuel Smith was taking charge of Baltimore's defenses, while Commander Major George Armistead bolstered men and ammunition at Fort McHenry. "The spirit of the nation is roused," the *Niles Register* of Baltimore proudly proclaimed.

THE STAR SPANGLED BANNER.

CURRIER AND IVES DEPICT THE US FLAG AND LADY LIBERTY, BETWEEN 1856 AND 1907. LIBRARY OF CONGRESS.

As seemingly numerous as the stars, fifteen thousand militia, volunteers, and regulars—young and old, Anglo and African—were making their way to defend Baltimore and Fort McHenry.

In contrast, less than four thousand men had hastily gathered to defend Washington, DC at Bladensburg, Maryland, before the British military burned the nation's capital city on August 24, 1814.

Charles Ingersoll, a congressman from Philadelphia at the time, would later describe these volunteers as symbols of the next generation. "The smoldering fires of the Capitol were spices of the phoenix bed, from which arose offspring more vigorous, beautiful, and long lived."

How brightly these stars would shine would soon become known. What or who shines brightly in your life today?

☆☆☆☆☆☆☆☆☆☆☆☆☆☆☆☆☆☆☆☆☆☆☆☆

I will make your descendants as numerous as the stars
in the sky and will give them all these lands, and through
your offspring all nations on earth will be blessed.
Genesis 26:4 (NIV)

☆☆☆☆☆☆☆☆☆☆☆☆☆☆☆☆☆☆☆☆☆☆☆☆

— 7 —

Through the Perilous Fight

George Washington told his men before the Battle of Long Island decades earlier in the late summer of 1776 that: "The fate of unborn millions will now depend, under God, on the courage and conduct of this army." He knew that they weren't just fighting for their own families, but also for the stars to come.

Can a fight ever be good? Can a fight ever be just? General Washington thought so, as he explained to his brother in December 1776, a few days before his army famously crossed the Delaware River: "However, under a full persuasion of the justice of our cause, I cannot entertain an idea that it will finally sink, tho' it may remain for some time under a cloud."

The same could be said for Francis Scott Key, who witnessed two fights during his mission to free Dr. Beanes. One was a shipboard quarrel of sorts. The other was the Battle of Fort McHenry.

When Key and Skinner arrived at the British flagship on September 7, 1814,

Admiral Cochrane was about to sit for dinner. He invited them to join him, along with General Ross and other British officers.

Their awkwardly polite conversation quickly deteriorated. An English officer insulted America. Skinner hurled back.

"Never was a man more disappointed in his expectations than I have been as to the character of British officers. With some exceptions they appeared to be illiberal, ignorant, and vulgar, and seem filled with a spirit of malignity against everything American," Key reflected.

With the duel of oral jabs going nowhere, General Ross offered to speak with Skinner privately. Though left out, Key was pleased with the outcome. Ross believed that Dr. Beanes had violated a gentleman's agreement with him to stay out of the fight when he seized the unruly British straggler. Yet, Ross agreed to free the physician during his private discussion with Skinner. Why? Evidence of goodwill. Skinner and Key had brought letters from injured British soldiers praising the good care provided by the Americans. President Madison had suggested the tactic.

"I shall accordingly give directions for his [Beanes's] being released ... but purely in proof of the obligation which I feel for the attention with which the wounded have been treated," Ross explained.

There was a catch. The American trio couldn't leave anytime soon, as the commanding admiral relayed.

"Ah, Mr. Skinner, after discussing so freely our preparation and plans, you could hardly expect us to let you go on shore in advance of us?" Cochrane retorted.

Hence, Key, Skinner, and Beanes would have to stay with the British fleet through the perilous battle to come.

☆☆☆☆☆☆☆☆☆☆☆☆☆☆☆☆☆☆☆☆☆☆☆☆☆

*I have fought the good fight, I have
finished the race, I have kept the faith.
2 Timothy 4:7 (NIV)*

☆☆☆☆☆☆☆☆☆☆☆☆☆☆☆☆☆☆☆☆☆☆☆☆☆

An 1812-era cannon points at the water from Fort McHenry. ©Jane Hampton Cook, www.janecook.com.

— 8 —

O'er the Ramparts We Watched

One reason that the British Army invaded Washington, DC on August 24, 1814, was the lack of an American defense. Focused on winning battles in Canada, General John Armstrong, the US war secretary, had ignored the fact that a British Admiral, George Cockburn, had been raiding Chesapeake Bay towns in Maryland and Virginia since 1813.

Prior to the August 1814 invasion, the war secretary had rejected pleas by local Washington residents to erect a battery at a nearby fort and call up regional militia on a rotating, twenty-four hour basis. As a result, the British marched more than forty miles from their ships toward the nation's capital with scarcely a shot fired at them, bridge burned, or road obstructed to stop their progress.

When asked if the British military would come to Washington, DC, Armstrong scoffed. "No, no! Baltimore is the place, Sir, that is of so much more consequence!" As the nation's third largest city, Baltimore was more commercially lucrative than Washington. British admirals also hated Baltimore because many of its private citizens had successfully harassed their ships. The British planned to go to Baltimore, but struck Washington first because they concluded it was an easier target and more symbolic of American principles.

Reflecting on his captivity with the British fleet, Key was worried about Baltimore. "To make my feelings still more acute, the admiral had intimated his fears that the town [Baltimore] must be burned, and I was sure that if taken it would have been given up to plunder ... It was filled with women and children."

While Key wondered when and if he, Skinner, and Beanes would be freed, the people of Baltimore were preparing for an attack. They were ramping up ramparts—defensive barriers. Mud hills. Cut trees. Hay stacks. All sorts of earthen works formed a mile-long barrier on the road leading to Baltimore at Hampstead Hill.

Likewise the super stars of Baltimore sank their ships to make navigating the waters more difficult for the larger British vessels. A line of armed barges also protected the harbor. People gave wagons and pickaxes. Banks contributed more than $660,000. One commander, John Rodgers, wrote proudly, "Forts, redoubts, and entrenchments are thrown up all round the town and the place now has nothing to fear, even should the enemy make his appearance tomorrow."

Wars can't be won without a defense. Nor can they be fought only on offense.

So it is with ordinary things in life. Football and many other sports can't be played with only an offense. They require defense, too. But a defense can't just be a barrier. It needs a logical plan, a strategy, to succeed.

☆☆☆☆☆☆☆☆☆☆☆☆☆☆☆☆☆☆☆☆☆☆☆☆☆

Walk about Zion, go around her, count her towers,
consider well her ramparts, view her citadels, that
you may tell of them to the next generation.
Psalm 48:12-13 (NIV)

☆☆☆☆☆☆☆☆☆☆☆☆☆☆☆☆☆☆☆☆☆☆☆☆☆

The flag gallantly waves. US Department of Defense, Wikimedia Commons Public Domain.

— 9 —

Were So Gallantly Streaming

*W*hat does gallantly mean to you? How about unflinching? Undaunted? Stouthearted in spirit? When have you seen that attitude in someone you admire?

Baltimore was streaming with armed men ready to fight in September 1814. One commander put it this way: "The people now begin to show something like a patriotic spirit. They are fortifying the town by all the means in their power … are pledged to me to defend the place to the last extremity."

The enemy was ready, too. On September 12, 1814, around 3 AM, British General Robert Ross and Admiral George Cockburn landed with four thousand men at North Point, outside of Baltimore. By mid-day, teenage American snipers had shot and killed Ross, who'd led an advance party in the forest and commanded the land forces. Though the British lost General Ross and more men than the Americans, they were still considered the victors of the land battle that day because the Americans retreated. The nearby US barricades, however, on Hampstead Hill forced the British to camp and carefully consider their next move. After their retreat, the Americans regrouped—a sign of progress and newfound determination.

Key was on a ship less than three miles away. How did he know what was going on behind the ramparts? He likely didn't, but he knew the attitude behind them.

Because he had been in Baltimore several days earlier, he'd caught a glimpse of the awakened spirit. He'd heard the outrage. He saw what he didn't see on August 24. With the Georgetown militia, he'd taken up arms at the Battle of Bladensburg. Though the Americans had fired a cannon at the bridge, the redcoats had scaled the hill and engaged in hand-to-hand combat.

Retreat had spread like wildfire through the American lines.

☆☆☆☆☆☆☆☆☆☆☆☆☆☆☆☆☆☆☆☆☆☆☆

They only saw a gallant show
Of heroes stalwart under banners,
And, in the fierce heroic glow,
'Twas theirs to yield but wild hosannas.
"Picciola" Robert Henry Newell
(1836-1901)

☆☆☆☆☆☆☆☆☆☆☆☆☆☆☆☆☆☆☆☆☆☆☆

And so Key had seen and participated in the fiasco scorned as the "Bladensburg Races." Men had trampled away as fast as horses on a racetrack. Back in England, newspapers bragged: "Washington is no more" and "the reign of [President] Madison may be considered as at an end."

The aftermath, however, had led to a renewal of patriotism. "The immediate and enthusiastic effect of the fall of Washington was electrical revival of national spirit and universal energy," Congressman Charles Ingersoll reflected. "It

was an attack, not against the strength or the resources of a state, but against the national honor and public affections of a people."

Key had seen that spirit come alive in Baltimore before voyaging with Skinner to the British fleet. People were more unflinching, stouthearted, and undaunted. Independence was on the line, and they weren't going to let it go without a fight.

Gallant can also mean something else. It's being attentive, while also adding respect, grace, and dignity to one's actions. Key saw the electric revival of the patriotic spirit—streaming gallantly like a fountain in Baltimore.

Fireworks soar over Fort McHenry. US Navy, Wikimedia Commons Public Domain.

— 10 —

And the Rockets' Red Glare

*W*hat leaves you in suspense? A movie thriller? A mystery novel? Waiting for the next release of a mobile phone or the newest technological wonder? For Francis Scott Key, suspense was watching the bombardment of Fort McHenry for more than twenty-four hours by rockets and bombs.

The morning of September 13, 1814, Key knew something big was happening. Admiral Cochrane ordered him and Skinner back onto the truce boat that they'd used to find the fleet several days earlier. Dr. Beanes now joined them, while a nearby armed British ship kept them from departing.

Sure enough, around 5 AM, Cochrane ordered several vessels to move into a line facing Fort McHenry two and three-quarter miles away. Soon the order came. Fire! Quickly realizing that the ships were too far away from the fort, the admiral sent them forward until they were two miles away. Return fire from the Americans soon led Cochrane to stop his advance. His ships couldn't safely move any closer. They'd have to rely on their rockets to do their job as best as possible.

From his position less than three miles away, Key could hear the shots. Aided by a spyglass, he could also see them—the latest in warfare technology: Congreve rockets.

William Congreve, a British engineer, had developed these weapons based on the ones fighters in India had hurled against the British in a war a few years earlier. Cone-shaped cylinders served as warheads. Sailors and marines attached them to four-foot wooden poles. The British then launched these rockets from metal A-shaped frames. By changing the elevation of the launching frames, they could adjust the distance of the rockets, which could go as far as two miles. These weapons also left a red glare in the sky, which made them a scary sight to behold.

For sixteen months British marines had used these Congreve rockets to burn houses along the Chesapeake Bay in terrorizing raids led by Admiral Cockburn. They also had used long poles to burn the White House. Lighting the ends of their poles, which contained plate-sized balls of oily rags, and standing in front of the windows and doors, the men had thrust their fiery sticks into the White House in unison, causing an instant ball of flames.

They didn't have the same luck on September 13, 1814. Within about two and a half hours after firing the rockets at Fort McHenry, the British pace slackened. Why?

US artillery had ripped one rocket ship's main sail, forcing the vessel to retreat.

Regrouping, the remaining ships continued firing, however. Such was the staccato suspense that Key, Skinner, and Beanes witnessed from their truce boat, trapped by the British fleet.

☆☆☆☆☆☆☆☆☆☆☆☆☆☆☆☆☆☆☆☆☆☆☆☆☆☆

What is glory?--in the socket
See how dying tapers fare!
What is pride?--a whizzing rocket
That would emulate a star.
"Inscriptions Supposed to be Found
in and near a Hermit's Cell"
William Wordsworth, 1770-1850

☆☆☆☆☆☆☆☆☆☆☆☆☆☆☆☆☆☆☆☆☆☆☆☆☆☆

Defenses surround Fort McHenry. © Jane Hampton Cook.

— 11 —

The Bombs Bursting in Air

When was the last time you sat on the edge of your seat in a movie theater or in your favorite chair at home and watched a heart-pounding chase scene in a movie? Minutes can seem like hours. Usually these sequences are a big-bang whirl of loud noises, buzzes, special effects, and crashes. You can hardly wait for the tension to ease and the movie to end—for the sun to rise, so to speak.

People often play back-to-back episodes of their favorite TV shows over several hours. Imagine watching the most suspenseful scenes from an intense TV show constantly for over twenty-four hours without resolution. That is what it was like for Mr. Key, Mr. Skinner, and Dr. Beanes as they beheld the bomb blasts during the bombardment of Fort McHenry. They were dying for the reality show to end.

Five British bomb ships hurled multiple bombs per hour in a nearly rhythmic pattern. The bombs' spherical ten- and thirteen-inch shells spread shrapnel.

Some bombs fell short; others went long. Some rained directly over the fort during the showers and squalls that also blasted the area. One US commander guessed that the British were "expending many rounds of shot from 1,800 to 2,000 shells and at least seven or eight hundred rockets."

Key had no idea what was going on inside Fort McHenry. He also didn't know that the British commanders were agonizing over the situation of their land forces. General Ross's death had dispirited them and left Colonel Arthur Brooke in command.

"It is for Colonel Brooke to consider under such circumstances whether he has force sufficient to defeat so large a number as it [is] said the enemy has collected; say twenty-thousand strong or even a less number and to take the town," Admiral Cochrane explained in a letter that he dispatched to Admiral Cockburn, who had been with Ross when he died and was with Brooke on the ground at the time. Because the Americans outnumbered them, Cochrane feared that they "will be only throwing the men's lives away" if they chose to attack.

Cochrane had also sent a captain and twenty vessels to try to land and distract the US forces defending the land redoubts. If the captain was successful, then Brooke would have a better chance to attack. But Brooke remained doubtful. He worried about the casualties they would incur if they advanced.

It seemed that many—both Americans and Britons—longed for sunlight to bring them out of the darkness of battle.

☆☆☆☆☆☆☆☆☆☆☆☆☆☆☆☆☆☆☆☆☆☆☆☆

Wouldst thou be free?
The chains that gall thy breast.
With one strong effort burst,
and be at rest.
"Of Nature in Men"
Francis Bacon (1561–1626)

☆☆☆☆☆☆☆☆☆☆☆☆☆☆☆☆☆☆☆☆☆☆☆☆

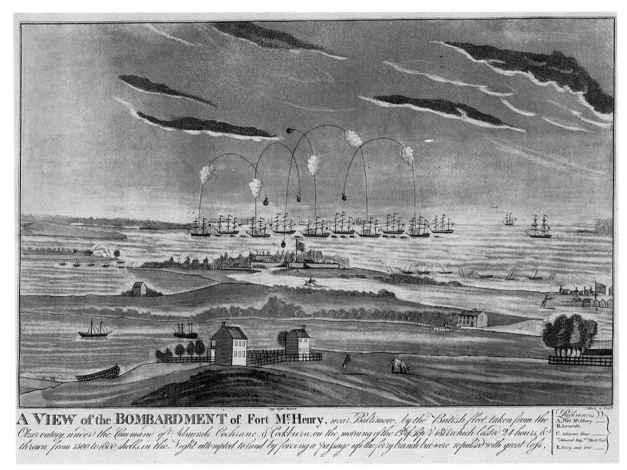

A VIEW of the BOMBARDMENT of Fort McHenry, near Baltimore, by the British fleet, taken from the Observatory, under the Command of Admirals Cochrane & Cockburn, on the morning of the 13th of Sep.r 1814 which lasted 24 hours, & thrown from 1500 to 1800 shells, in the Night attempted to land by forcing a passage up the ferry branch but were repulsed with great loss.

AN ARTIST DEPICTS THE BOMBARDMENT OF FORT MCHENRY, JOHN BOWER, 1819, LIBRARY OF CONGRESS.

— 12 —

Gave Proof through the Night

*T*angible evidence guides and affects us throughout life. Sometimes it's a negative indicator. A mistake on a multiple choice test lowers a final grade. A thermometer's elevated temperature means fever, which indicates sickness. A police camera catches a car driver running a red light.

Sometimes evidence is positive and hopeful. The scales show lost weight, leading to better health. The sales report reveals an upward trend, indicating more revenue for the business. The pregnancy test pops a plus sign, showing that new life is coming.

Because he was an attorney, Francis Scott Key was well versed in the value of evidence. As one who oversaw estate sales, he needed proof that his clients owned the land they were selling. Deeds and legal papers were essential to his business. It was also papers of proof that had freed Dr. Beanes. Letters from wounded British soldiers had proved that the Americans were treating them humanely.

It makes sense that Key kept his eye on the evidence during the sleepless night of September 13 and the early morning of September 14. While bombs burst and rockets branded the black sky red, he kept his eye on Fort McHenry.

Months earlier, Commander Armistead had ordered the creation of a flag measuring seventeen by twenty-five feet to serve as the fort's battle or storm flag. Local flag maker, Mary Pickersgill, had fulfilled his request.

Throughout the night under the thundering bombardment by the British, Key looked to hope and faith that Fort McHenry would not fall.

Yet, just as the bombs flew that night, many questions also could have pounded his mind. What would happen if the Americans lost this battle? If the British conquered Baltimore, wouldn't they go to Philadelphia next? Then New York? Boston? Now that England's war with France had recently ended, couldn't the British government send twenty thousand or more soldiers and sailors to America's shores? Was the United States soon to be no more?

Then suddenly, the rhythm of bombs and rockets and return fire stopped. Replacing it was silence. With that silence came the disappearance of Fort McHenry's battle flag. What would replace it? What would Key see next through his spyglass? Please, don't let it be the white flag of surrender or the broad stripes of Britain's Union Jack. Neither was a sight that he could bear to behold.

DAWN GREETS THE RESTORED US CAPITOL. ©JENNIFER DAVIS HEFFNER, WWW.VITAIMAGES.COM.

☆☆☆☆☆☆☆☆☆☆☆☆☆☆☆☆☆☆☆☆☆☆☆☆☆☆☆☆☆☆

The wind that sighs before the dawn, chases the gloom of night,
The curtains of the East are drawn, and suddenly—'t is light.
Le Vent de l'Esprit, Sir Lewis Morris (1833-1907)

☆☆☆☆☆☆☆☆☆☆☆☆☆☆☆☆☆☆☆☆☆☆☆☆☆☆☆☆☆☆

A REPLICA OF THE STAR-SPANGLED BANNER FLAG FLIES AT FORT MCHENRY, ©JANE HAMPTON COOK, WWW.JANECOOK.COM.

In fine, the war, with all its vicissitudes, is illustrating the capacity and the destiny of the United States to be a great, a flourishing, and a powerful nation, worthy of the friendship … ~James Madison

— 13 —

That Our Flag Was Still There

*W*hat does silence mean to you? Is it glorious? Peaceful? Suspenseful? Uncomfortable? Silence can mean many things, depending on the context. Silence is golden, however, when it comes after a time of noise. The louder, more agonizing the noise, the more welcome the quiet.

Suddenly, through the silence, Key saw them—the most beautiful colors in the world. The largest US flag he'd ever seen burst to the top of the pole at Fort McHenry by the dawn's early light. This sight could only mean one thing. Fort McHenry remained in American hands.

Earlier in the year, Commander Armistead had not only commissioned the smaller storm flag for Fort McHenry, but he'd also ordered "a flag so large that the British will have no difficulty in seeing it from a distance." Flag maker Mary Pickersgill had crafted both. The giant flag stretched thirty feet by forty-two feet. Its stars alone measured twenty-four inches from point to point.

What Key didn't know was that one thousand men had come to Fort McHenry.

Refusing to give in, Commander Armistead and his forces held their ground, firing back. Miraculously only four had been killed, even though Armistead thought as many as fifteen hundred weapons had reached the fort.

In addition, British Admiral Cochrane's attempt to send a captain and nearly two dozen vessels to aid Colonel Brooke on land had failed. Seeing them, an American opened fire, stopping their assault. Brooke concluded that the stakes were too high. Continuing the land assault would result in the loss of too many lives. He couldn't live the rest of his life wondering if he'd needlessly thrown away the lives of men, like tossing leaves to the wind. Instead, he ordered the British forces to retreat. Back to the boats. It was time to go.

Commander John Rodgers described the enemy's departure this way: "The enemy has been severely drubbed, as well his army as his navy, and is now retiring down the river."

As a few men raised the large flag over Fort McHenry, others fired their guns in a victory salute while still others played *Yankee Doodle*. Suddenly the silence gave way to song.

Visitors help to lower and fold the replica of the Star-Spangled Banner flag, measuring 30 x 42 feet, at Fort McHenry. © Jane Hampton Cook.

— 14 —

O Say, Does that Star-Spangled Banner Yet Wave

*S*oon Francis Scott Key, John Skinner, and Dr. William Beanes were free, too. Anchors aweigh they went. Somewhere during their return voyage, or perhaps during the battle, Key's emotions took flight; so much so that he had to write down what was in his heart.

Poetic words came to his mind in a rhythmic pattern. Perhaps the phrases came like a flood, raining so fast that it was hard to catch them with pen and paper. Or maybe they came in bits and pieces, like a puzzle pulsing to conform to a cadence. However it happened, came they did.

Up first was the introduction. "O say, can you see, by the dawn's early light, what so proudly we hailed at the twilight's last gleaming?" Next was the nation's most recognizable symbol: "Whose broad stripes and bright stars, through the perilous fight." Then came the heroes: "O'er the ramparts we watched, were so gallantly streaming!" He couldn't forget the bombardment, the dark night of soul. "And the rockets' red glare, the bombs bursting in air."

The suspense and endurance "gave proof through the night that our flag was still there." When Key was finished with his lyrics, he had created something with a dual effect. His song clearly represented what happened at the *Defence of Fort McHenry*, the song's original name. But Fort McHenry did more than represent a city. It symbolized America. The giant flag didn't just soar over Baltimore, it unfurled over the entire United States. "O say, does that star-spangled banner yet wave, O'er the land of the free and the home of the brave?" It is no surprise that the song became known as *The Star-Spangled Banner*.

Key's word pattern fit the tune *To Anacreon in Heaven*, a melody he'd used a few years earlier to write another song. The music was also well known to many Americans as the *Boston Patriotic Song* or the *Adams and Liberty Song*,

FRANCIS SCOTT KEY WITNESSES THE BATTLE OF FORT MCHENRY. LIBRARY OF CONGRESS.

written to celebrate the presidency of John Adams years earlier. Originating from the Anacreontic Society, which was a club in England, the tune was named after Anacreon, a lyric poet from Greece.

What started with the burning of the US Capitol and the White House at the twilight's last gleaming gave birth to a new dawn for Americans and a new song for the nation.

What's your favorite song? Who or what puts a song in your heart?

☆☆☆☆☆☆☆☆☆☆☆☆☆☆☆☆☆☆☆☆☆☆☆☆☆☆

Who is this that appears like the dawn,
fair as the moon, bright as the sun,
majestic as the stars in procession?
Song of Songs 6:10

☆☆☆☆☆☆☆☆☆☆☆☆☆☆☆☆☆☆☆☆☆☆☆☆☆☆

A boy holds the US flag. © Paul Ernest, www.paulernest.com.

The Star-Spangled Banner flag displayed at the National Museum of American History in Washington, DC. Smithsonian Institution Archives, Wikimedia Commons Public Domain.

— 15 —

O'er the Land of the Free

*H*ow often have you heard *The Star-Spangled Banner*? Hundreds of times, most likely, in this land of the free. From baseball and football games to school assemblies and Independence Day fireworks, the song is an integral part of America.

While the first verse is well known, four verses poured from Francis Scott Key's pen, including lesser-sung flourishes: "O thus be it ever, when freemen shall stand, between their loved homes and the war's desolation!"

Some phrases reflect faith: "Blest with victory and peace, may the heaven-rescued land praise the power that hath made and preserved us a nation."

One phrase in particular stands out because it put into print, perhaps for the first time, a common sentiment from Key's and the founding era: "And this be our motto: 'In God is our trust.'" Little did Key know that years later his words would be engraved on US coins. Each verse ended with the refrain: "O'er the land of the free and the home of the brave!"

Key arrived in Baltimore on September 16, 1814, and spent the night at the Indian Queen Hotel. He shared his new lyrics with Judge Joseph Nicholson, one of his brothers-in-law who'd led a unit to defend Baltimore. Tapping his connections, Nicholson arranged to publish Key's poem as a broadside, which was a large poster hung in public locations.

Including Key's hometown paper in Georgetown, soon newspapers around the nation—the land of the free—printed the poem, albeit anonymously.

☆☆☆☆☆☆☆☆☆☆☆☆☆☆☆☆☆☆☆☆☆☆☆☆

... Proclaim liberty throughout the land to all its inhabitants ...
Leviticus 25:10 (NIV)

☆☆☆☆☆☆☆☆☆☆☆☆☆☆☆☆☆☆☆☆☆☆☆☆

A few weeks later, Key wrote his story in a letter to a congressman and political opponent of President Madison. Key also shared what happened with his children and, later, his grandchildren, who wrote it down and kept his memory alive.

What does the land of the free mean to you? An important quality to Key's lyrics is their universal meaning. Though he wrote a song that described the Battle of Fort McHenry, his words weren't so specific that they couldn't be applied to both past and future situations.

General Marquis de Lafayette could have sung similar words at the end of the Battle of Yorktown, the last major battle of the Revolutionary War, when he realized that his troops had succeeded in defeating the enemy. Similar sentiment filled events and parades celebrating the end of the Civil War, World War II, and others.

While Key saw that his song of liberty resonated with his generation, he had no idea what would happen to it in the years to come in the land of the free and the home of the brave.

This flag was used to cover fallen fire fighters on Sept. 11, 2001. US Navy Wikimedia Commons Public Domain.

US Airmen salute the flag. US Dept. of Defense, Wikimedia Commons Public Domain.

— 16 —

And the Home of the Brave

Can you better see what Francis Scott Key saw the morning of September 14, 1814? Do you better understand the emotions he felt, knowing that the star-spangled banner would continue to wave in the future because of the patriotism displayed by people in Baltimore?

Within a few months, the war officially ended. John Quincy Adams and the other US peace negotiators signed the Treaty of Ghent, the treaty ending the war, on December 24, 1814. Without knowledge of the treaty, two weeks later General Andrew Jackson defeated British forces in New Orleans on January 8, 1815. President Madison signed the treaty in February 1815.

Commander Armistead saved the large flag that had flown at Fort McHenry as a memento of the battle. "It is always such a satisfaction to me to feel that the flag is just where it is, in possession for all time of the very best custodian, where it is beautifully displayed and can be conveniently seen by so many people," he explained.

Armistead also gave away pieces of the flag to others who revered it. Later the flag was attached to canvas. It was displayed and photographed for the first time at the Boston Navy Yard in 1873. By 1907, this very fragile flag was given to the Smithsonian Institution in Washington, DC, where it was preserved using standards of the day.

While Key's song was popular during his lifetime, he never experienced the celebrity that came after his death. As the home of the brave expanded west, the song became one of the most popular patriotic tunes in America, especially during the Civil War. By the 1890s, *The Star-Spangled Banner* was a military requirement, to be played during flag raising and lowering ceremonies. By 1917, the US Army and US Navy declared it the national anthem for ceremonial occasions. President William Taft and Helen Taft marched to it on their twenty-fifth wedding anniversary at the White House in 1911.

The Star-Spangled Banner became the focus of several campaigns by patriotic groups determined to make it America's official national anthem. Congress and the president finally did just that. Designating *The Star-Spangled Banner* as the nation's official song, President Herbert Hoover signed it into law on March 3, 1931. The home of the brave now had an anthem for the ages.

After being displayed in the hall of the Smithsonian's National Museum of American History in Washington, DC since 1964, the Star-Spangled Banner flag was removed for preservation in 1998. Experts attached a lightweight polyester backing to allow it to be displayed in a new state-of-the art climate- and light-controlled preservation lab at the museum for visitors to see.

☆☆☆☆☆☆☆☆☆☆☆☆☆☆☆☆☆☆☆☆☆☆☆

You brave heroic minds
Worthy your country's name,
That honour still pursue;
Go and subdue!
"To the Virginian Voyage"
Michael Drayton (1563–1631)

☆☆☆☆☆☆☆☆☆☆☆☆☆☆☆☆☆☆☆☆☆☆☆

The flag and song were united for the first time on June 14, 2014, when a copy of the lyrics to *The Star-Spangled Banner* in Key's handwriting was displayed with the flag at the museum. *The Star-Spangled Banner* celebrated its 200th birthday on September 13-14, 2014, an anniversary for the ages.

What do you see and feel when you hear the nation's song? No matter the generation, America's star-spangled story is a great source of pride, one to be remembered and passed along to others. O say can you see?

AMERICANS SING THE NATIONAL ANTHEM AND SALUTE THE US MILITARY. ©JENNIFER DAVIS HEFFNER, WWW.VITAIMAGES.COM.

— 17 —

Lyrics to The Star-Spangled Banner
by Francis Scott Key

O say can you see, by the dawn's early light,

What so proudly we hail'd at the twilight's last gleaming,

Whose broad stripes and bright stars through the perilous fight

O'er the ramparts we watch'd were so gallantly streaming?

And the rocket's red glare, the bombs bursting in air,

Gave proof through the night that our flag was still there,

O say does that star-spangled banner yet wave

O'er the land of the free and the home of the brave?

On the shore dimly seen through the mists of the deep

Where the foe's haughty host in dread silence reposes,

What is that which the breeze, o'er the towering steep,

As it fitfully blows, half conceals, half discloses?
Now it catches the gleam of the morning's first beam,
In full glory reflected now shines in the stream,
'Tis the star-spangled banner - O long may it wave
O'er the land of the free and the home of the brave!

And where is that band who so vauntingly swore,
That the havoc of war and the battle's confusion
A home and a Country should leave us no more?
Their blood has wash'd out their foul footstep's pollution.
No refuge could save the hireling and slave
From the terror of flight or the gloom of the grave,
And the star-spangled banner in triumph doth wave
O'er the land of the free and the home of the brave.

O thus be it ever when freemen shall stand
Between their lov'd home and the war's desolation!
Blest with vict'ry and peace may the heav'n rescued land
Praise the power that hath made and preserv'd us a nation!

Then conquer we must, when our cause it is just,
And this be our motto - "In God is our trust,"
And the star-spangled banner in triumph shall wave
O'er the land of the free and the home of the brave.

By order of the president of the United States, Fort McHenry flies a US flag twenty-four hours a day, including a replica of The Star-Spangled Banner Flag.
©Jane Hampton Cook, www.janecook.com.

— 18 —

Bibliography

"Fort McHenry." National Park Service, http://www.nps.gov/fomc/historyculture/the-great-garrison-flag.htm.

Bacon, Francis. *Essays, Civil and Moral. Vol. III, Part 1. The Harvard Classics.* New York: P.F. Collier & Son, 1909–14; http://www.Bartleby.com, 2001.

Bartlett, John. *Familiar Quotations, 10th ed*, rev. and enl. by Nathan Haskell Dole. Boston: Little, Brown, 1919; http://www.Bartleby.com, 2000.

Dudley, William S. *The Naval War of 1812: A Documentary History Vol. II 1813.* Naval Historical Center Department of the Navy, Washington, DC, 1992.

Federal Republican-Georgetown, Sept. 1, 1814, http://www.Genealogybank.com.

George, Christopher T. *Terror on the Chesapeake.* White Mane Books: Pennsylvania, 2000.

Ingersoll, Charles Jared. *Historical Sketch of the Second War Between the United States of America and Great Britain*. Lea and Blanchard: Philadelphia, 1845.

Journal of the Continental Congress, Vol. 8, June 14, 1777. Library of Congress.

Ketcham, Ralph. *James Madison: A Biography*. University of Virginia Press: Charlottesville, 1990.

Key, Francis Scott. *How Francis Scott Key Wrote The Star-Spangled Banner*. http://www.usgennet.org/usa/topic/preservation/epochs/vol5/pg90.htm.

_____. Letter to Mrs. Ann Phoebe Key, Jan. 2, 1814, University of Virginia Special Collections.

Lord, Walter. *The Dawn's Early Light*. The Johns Hopkins University Press: Baltimore, 1994.

Madison, James. *Special Message to Congress*, June 1, 1812 http://millercenter.org/president/speeches/detail/3614.

_____. *The James Madison Papers*, Library of Congress, Manuscript Division, Washington, DC.

Marshall, John. *The Life of George Washington*, Vol. 2, The Citizen's Guild of Washington's Boyhood Home, Fredericksburg, VA, 1926.

Seale, William. *The President's House: a History*. Vol. 1 and 2. Washington, DC: The White House Historical Association with the cooperation of the National Geographic Society, 1986.

Shulman, Holly C., ed. *Dolley Madison Digital Edition*. University of Virginia: Charlottesville. http://rotunda.upress.virginia.edu/.

Stedman, Edmund Clarence, ed. *An American Anthology, 1787–1900*. Boston: Houghton Mifflin, 1900; Bartleby.com, 2001.

The Star-Spangled Banner. Smithsonian Institution. http://amhistory.si.edu/starspangledbanner/.

Van Ness, John. "Testimony, Communicated Nov. 23, 1814," *Capture of the City of Washington, 13th Congress Report*, http://www.loc.gov.

Washington, George. "Letter to Augustine Washington, Dec. 18, 1776," in *Hart's American History Contemporaries*, 559–60.

Wordsworth, William. *The Complete Poetical Works*. London: Macmillan and Co., 1888; http://www.Bartleby.com, 1999.

Quote Notes

Chapter 1: "There is a secret in life," Dolley Madison: *America's First Lady*, PBS, 2010.

Chapter 2: "Unless the country," *Federal Republican-Georgetown*, Sept. 1, 1814, Genealogybank.com.

Chapter 2: "I really think," Francis Key to Mrs. Ann Phoebe Key, Jan. 2, 1814, University of Virginia Special Collections.

Chapter 2: "When the dawn," George William Russell. *Collected Poems* by A.E. London, Macmillan, 1913. Bartleby.com, 2001.

Chapter 3: "yield to the claims," James Madison, *Special Message to Congress*, June 1, 1812 millercenter.org/president/speeches/detail/3614.

Chapter 3: "abominable war," Francis Scott Key to John Randolph, http://www.usgennet.org/usa/topic/preservation/epochs/vol5/pg90.htm.

Chapter 4: "destroying and laying waste," James Madison, Sept. 1, 1814, *Writings of James Madison*, 305.

Chapter 4: "The day was lingering," Edmund Clarence Stedman, ed. *A Victorian Anthology, 1837–1895*. Cambridge: Riverside Press, 1895; Bartleby.com, 2003.

Chapter 5: "That the flag," *Journal of the Continental Congress*, Vol. 8, June 14, 1777. Library of Congress.

Chapter 6: "The spirit of the," Walter Lord, *Dawn's Early Light*, 216-7.

Chapter 6: "That the union be," *Journal of the Continental Congress*, Vol. 8, June 14, 1777. Library of Congress.

Chapter 6: "The smoldering fires," Charles Ingersoll, *Historical Sketch*, 197.

Chapter 7: "The fate of unborn," John Marshall, *The Life of George Washington*, Vol. 2

Chapter 7: "However, under a full persuasion," George Washington, "Letter to Augustine Washington, Dec. 18, 1776," in *Hart's American History Contemporaries*, 559–60.

Chapter 7: "Never was a man," Walter Lord, *Dawn's Early Light*, 216-17.

Chapter 7: "I shall accordingly," Christopher George, *Terror on the Chesapeake,* note, 132.

Chapter 7: "Ah, Mr. Skinner," Walter Lord, *Dawn's Early Light,* 256.

Chapter 8: "No, no! Baltimore," *John Van Ness Testimony, Communicated Nov. 23, 1814, Capture of the City of Washington,* 13th Congress Report, 581.

Chapter 8: "To make my feelings," Francis Scott Key to John Randolph http://www.usgennet.org/usa/topic/preservation/epochs/vol5/pg90.htm.

Chapter 8: "Forts, redoubts," John Rodgers to Alexander Murray, *Naval War of 1812,* Vol. 3, Sept. 9, 1814, 263.

Chapter 9: "The people now begin," John Rodgers to William Jones, *Naval War of 1812,* Vol. 3, Aug. 29, 1814, 244.

Chapter 9: "Washington is no more," Walter Lord, *Dawn's Early Light,* 302.

Chapter 9: "The immediate," Charles Ingersoll, *Historical Sketch,* 197.

Chapter 9: "They only saw," Edmund Clarence Stedman, ed. *An American Anthology, 1787–1900.* Boston: Houghton Mifflin, 1900; Bartleby.com, 2001.

Chapter 10: "What is Glory?" William Wordsworth, *The Complete Poetical Works*. London: Macmillan and Co., 1888; Bartleby.com, 1999.

Chapter 11: "Expending many rounds," John Rodgers to William Jones, Sept. 14, 1814, *Naval War of 1812*, 293.

Chapter 11: "It is for Colonel Brooke," Admiral Cochrane to Admiral Cockburn, Sept. 13, 1814, *Naval War 1812*, Vol. 3, 277.

Chapter 11: "Wouldst thou be free?" Francis Bacon, *Essays, Civil and Moral*. Vol. III, Part 1. *The Harvard Classics*. New York: P.F. Collier & Son, 1909–14; Bartleby.com, 2001.

Chapter 12: "The wind that sighs," John Bartlett, comp. *Familiar Quotations*, 10th ed, rev. and enl. by Nathan Haskell Dole. Boston: Little, Brown, 1919; Bartleby.com, 2000.

Chapter 13: "In fine, the war," James Madison, Dec. 7, 1813, *Writings of James Madison*, 265.

Chapter 13: "The enemy has been," John Rodgers to William Jones, Sept. 14, 1814, *Naval War of 1812*, 293.

Chapter 13: "a flag so large," George Armistead, National Park Service, Fort McHenry http://www.nps.gov/fomc/historyculture/the-great-garrison-flag.htm.

Chapter 13: "O golden silence," John Bartlett, comp. *Familiar Quotations*, 10th ed, rev. and enl. by Nathan Haskell Dole. Boston: Little, Brown, 1919; www.bartleby.com/100/.

Chapter 14, 15, & 17: *Star-Spangled Banner* lyrics, Smithsonian's National Museum of American History, http://amhistory.si.edu/starspangledbanner/the-lyrics.aspx.

Chapter 16: "You brave heroic minds," Charles W. Eliot, ed. *English Poetry I: From Chaucer to Gray. Vol. XL. The Harvard Classics.* New York: P.F. Collier & Son, 1909–14; Bartleby.com, 2001.

About the Author

Jane Hampton Cook makes history relevant to news, politics, faith, and modern life. She is the award-winning author of eight books, including Pulitzer-nominated *American Phoenix*, which brings to life the international side of the War of 1812 through the diplomatic service of John Quincy and Louisa Adams. *Stories of Faith and Courage from the Revolutionary War* and *The Faith of America's First Ladies* are among her other titles.

A national media commentator and former White House webmaster, Jane is a frequent guest on the Fox News Channel and other television and radio outlets, including the History Channel's H2 network. She launched her passion for history and writing through a research fellowship from the Organization of American Historians and White House Historical Association. Jane and her husband, Dr. John Kim Cook, live with their children in the Washington, DC area in Fairfax, Virginia. *www. janecook.com.*

PHOTO BY JENNIFER DAVIS HEFFNER, VITAIMAGES.COM.

Made in the USA
Charleston, SC
12 July 2014